$23.60

MW01125691

OCT - - 2018

MAP MY
COMMUNITY

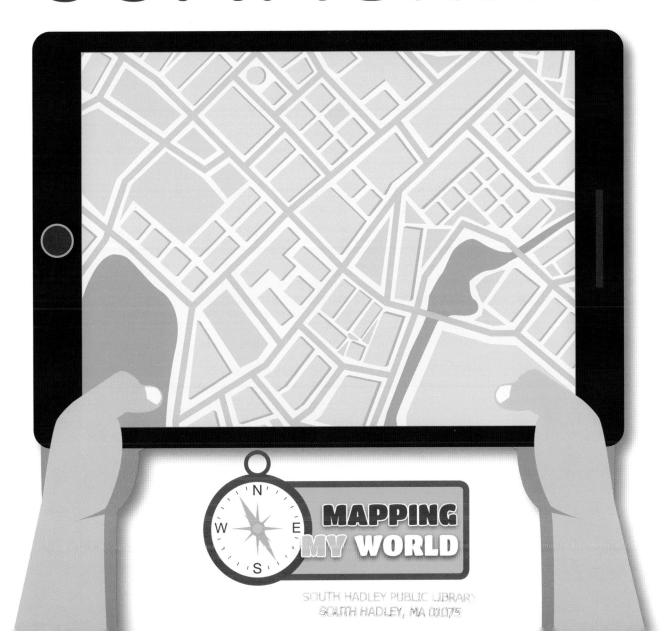

MAPPING
MY WORLD

CRABTREE
PUBLISHING COMPANY
WWW.CRABTREEBOOKS.COM

Published in Canada
Crabtree Publishing
616 Welland Avenue
St. Catharines, ON
L2M 5V6

Published in the United States
Crabtree Publishing
PMB 59051
350 Fifth Ave, 59th Floor
New York, NY 10118

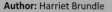

Published in 2019 by Crabtree Publishing Company

Author: Harriet Brundle

Editors: Kirsty Holmes, Kathy Middleton

Design: Matt Rumbelow

Proofreader: Janine Deschenes

Prepress technician: Tammy McGarr

Print coordinator: Katharine Berti

Photographs

Images are courtesy of Shutterstock.com. With thanks to Getty Images, Thinkstock Photo and iStockphoto. 2 –SkyPics Studio. 3 – Nadia Buravleva. 4 – DVARG. 5 – Vectorpocket. 6 – george studio. 7 – Bardocz Peter. 8: Incomible, Egret77, LuckyVector. 9 – Art Alex. 10: Sarunyu_foto, Dmitry Guzhanin. 11 – SkyPics Studio. 12 – nnnnae. 13: t – Shai_Halud, b – Ira Yapanda. 14 – veralub. 15 – Igogosha. 16 – German Icons. 17 – MatoomMi. 18 – Shai_Halud. 19 – turbodesign. 20 – Oxy_gen. 21 – Santitep Mongkolsin, dreamstale. 22 – Beresnev. 23 – Dark ink.

Printed in the U.S.A./082018/CG20180601

Library and Archives Canada Cataloguing in Publication

Brundle, Harriet, author
        Map my community / Harriet Brundle.

(Mapping my world)
Includes index.
Issued in print and electronic formats.
ISBN 978-0-7787-5001-7 (hardcover).
ISBN 978-0-7787-5012-3 (softcover).
ISBN 978-1-4271-2130-1 (HTML)

        1. Cartography--Juvenile literature. 2. Maps--Juvenile literature.
I. Title.

GA105.6.B78 2018   j526   C2018-902380-5
                                                   C2018-902381-3

Library of Congress Cataloging-in-Publication Data

CONTENTS

Words that look like **this** can be found in the glossary on page 24.

WHAT IS A MAP?

A map is a picture that gives us information about an area. Maps can show us a lot of different things. A map can show roads, stores, and transportation in a community. A community is a group of people who live in the same area and share services.

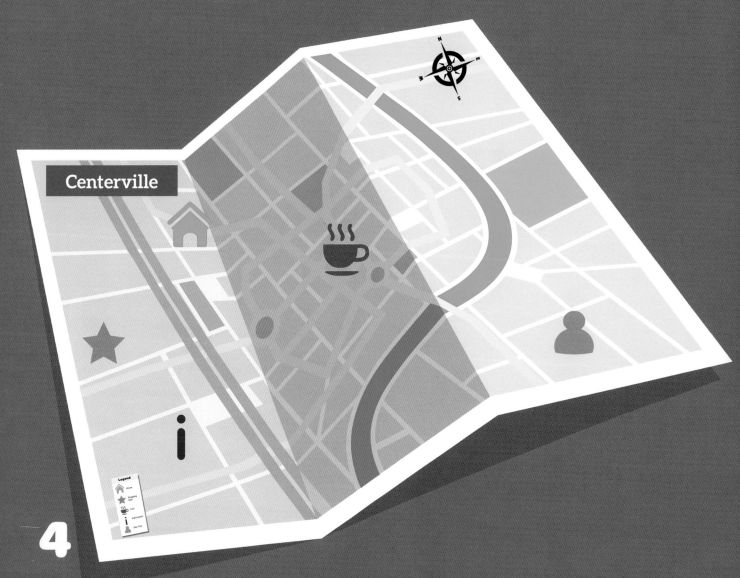

Centerville

Maps can be printed on paper or viewed on screens. Maps viewed on screens are called digital maps.

Digital Map

A map has a title. This helps the person who is reading it figure out what is on the map.

Centerville

Centerville

USING A MAP

It is hard to see an entire community when you are standing in one place. A map gives you something called a "bird's-eye view" of an area. A bird looking down from above could see more area than you could.

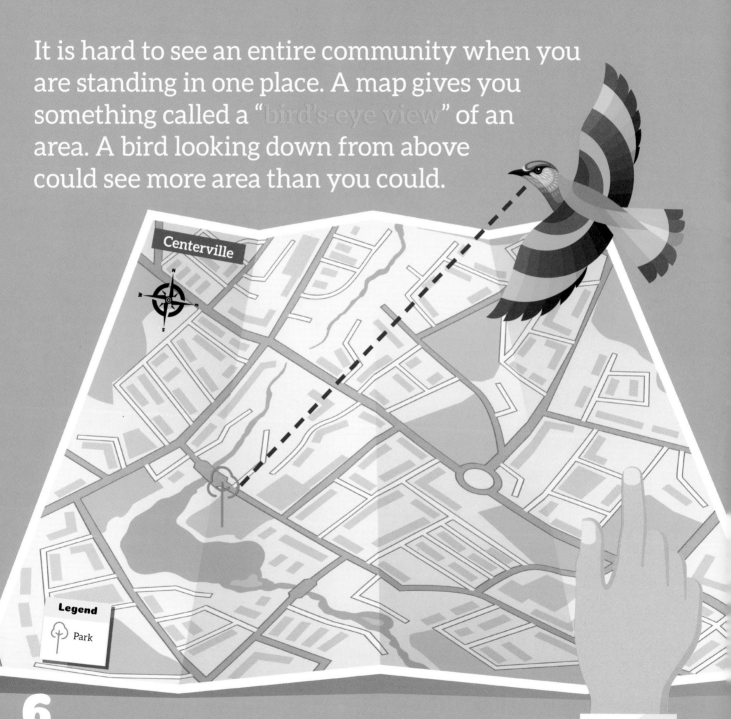

Centerville

Legend

🌳 Park

A map usually has a compass rose in the corner. The points on a compass rose are marked with the letters N, E, S, and W. The letters tell you which direction is north, south, east, or west.

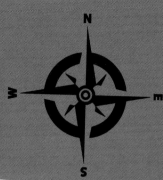

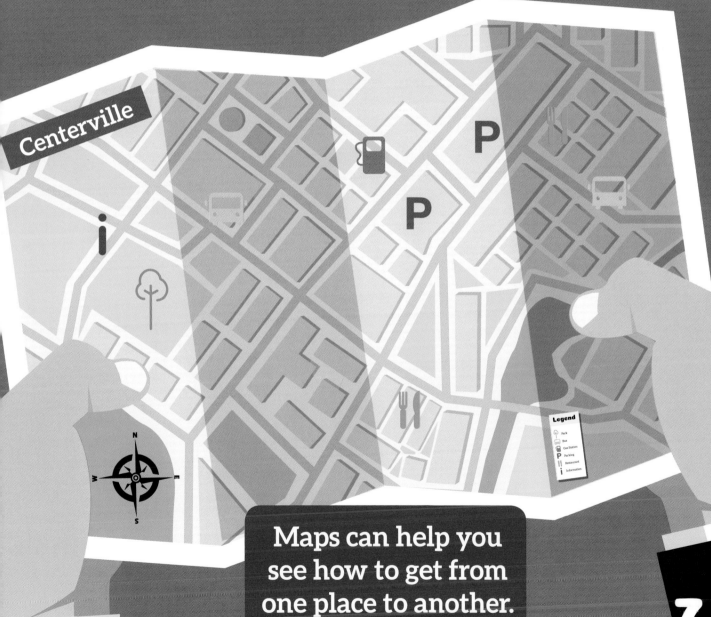

Centerville

Legend
- Park
- Bus
- Gas Station
- P Parking
- Restaurant
- Information

Maps can help you see how to get from one place to another.

LEGEND

Maps use colors and **symbols** to show you where important things are located. Symbols are pictures that stand for other things. A list of the colors and symbols and what they mean usually appears in the corner of a map. This list is called a **legend**.

Map of Centerville

Legend

PARK · PARKING · TELEPHONE

GAS STATION · ROAD · RESTAURANT

You might see symbols like this to show where a restaurant is located.

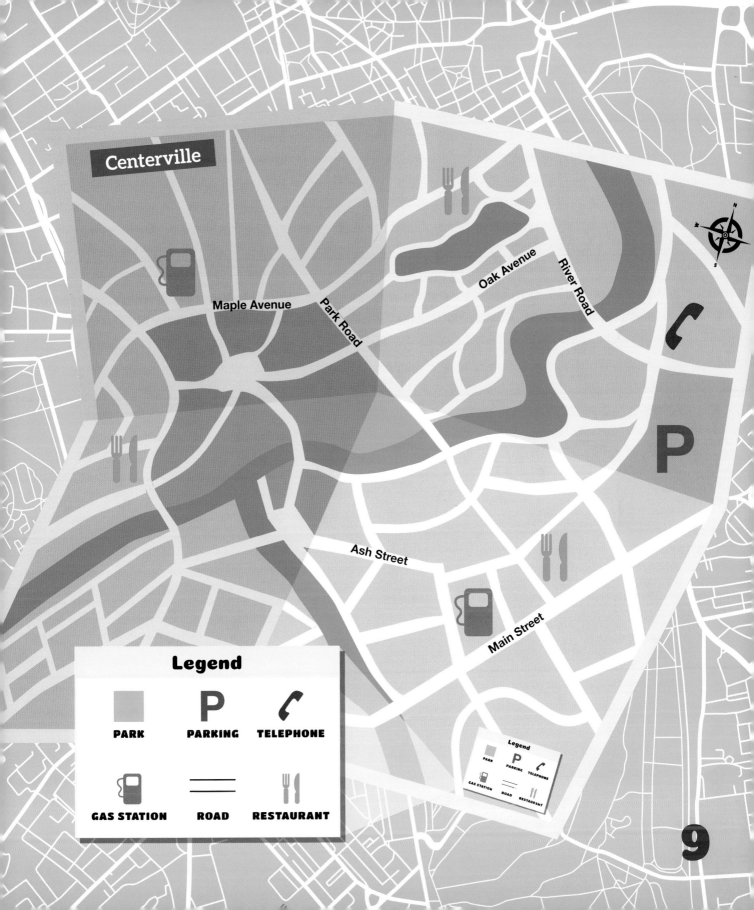

SCALE

An entire community is too big to show on a map at its real size. Everything on a map is made smaller by the same amount so it will fit on the paper or a screen. The amount it has been shrunk is called the scale.

Littleton

Legend

Golf Couse

Scale
1 inch = 100 feet
(2.5 centimeters = 30 meters)

Scale
1 inch = 100 feet
(2.5 centimeters = 30 meters)

The scale is found near the legend. You can use the scale on a map to figure out distance on the ground. To figure out the real distance between your home and the grocery store, measure the distance on the map with a ruler. Then multiply that number by the scale.

Chestnut
Grocery Store

Chestnut Street

Parker Street

Main Street

Scale
1 inch = 100 feet
(2.5 centimeters = 30 meters)

The distance between two points on a map stands for the real distance on the ground.

11

DIFFERENT MAPS

There are many different kinds of maps. Each kind shows different things.
A physical map shows landforms, which are the natural shapes of the land. Examples of landforms include rivers and mountains.

This is a political map. A political map shows the borders of an area. Borders are imaginary lines that divide areas into smaller parts. This map shows how South America is divided into countries.

Countries in South America

Venezuela
Colombia
Guyanna
Suriname
French Guiana
Brazil
Peru
Ecuador
Bolivia
Chile
Argentina
Paraguay
Uruguay

Street maps show the roads in a city or community. Some street maps show us all the points of interest in an area, too. These are places many people might like to visit. The map shows you which streets to follow to get from place to place.

DOWNTOWN CENTERVILLE

Scale
1 inch = 100 feet
(2.5 centimeters = 30 meters)

Legend
Airport
Bathroom
P Parking
Restaurant
Telephone

Stops for transportation, such as buses, are also shown on street maps.

13

WHO WOULD USE A STREET MAP?

You could use a street map! A map of your neighborhood or community would help you learn the names of local streets and help you get from place to place.

Visitors to a community who do not know their way around could find directions on a street map.

POINTS OF INTEREST
IN A COMMUNITY

A community has streets, homes, stores, and services used by the people who live there. A service is work people need to have done for them. What do you think these symbols might stand for on a community map?

Can you think of any other symbols a community map legend might need?

Try drawing a bird's-eye view of the street you live on. Draw squares for houses and rectangles for apartment buildings. Are there any parks or stores on your street?

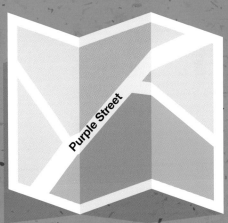

Purple Street

MAPPING MY COMMUNITY

Get a parent or caregiver to take you around the streets surrounding your house. Write down the names of the streets and which ones cross each other. Make a list of any special points of interest such as parks, corner stores, or bus stops.

DRAW THE STREETS

Draw a bird's-eye view of the streets on a sheet of paper or a digital device. Add the names of the streets.

Identify your house and the houses of friends and family in your neighborhood.

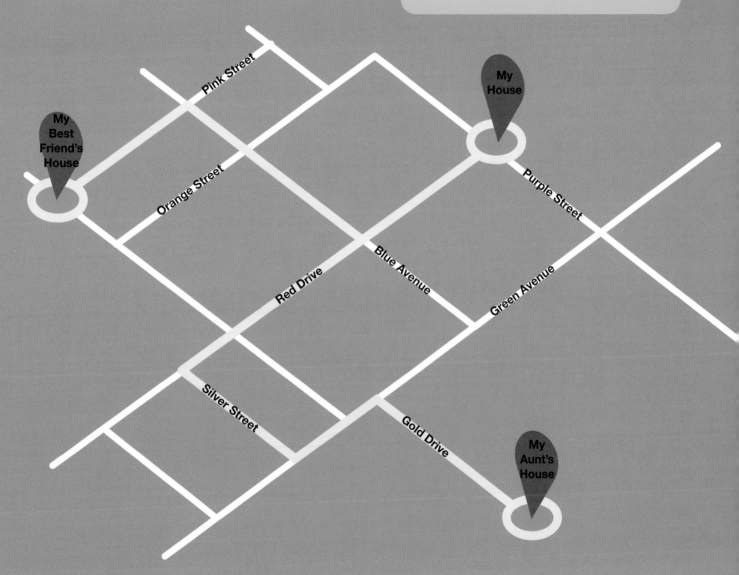

Pink Street

My Best Friend's House

Orange Street

Red Drive

Blue Avenue

My House

Purple Street

Green Avenue

Silver Street

Gold Drive

My Aunt's House

POINTS OF INTEREST

Create symbols for your list of points of interest. Don't forget to add anything in your community that is popular with visitors, such as a sports stadium.

Does your community have a market that sells local vegetables?

SHOP

COFFEE

CANDY SHOP

BARBER SHOP

STO

20

CREATE A LEGEND

Make a legend of your symbols. Check the list on page 16 to see if you need to add some from that list. Add the symbols to the map in the correct place.

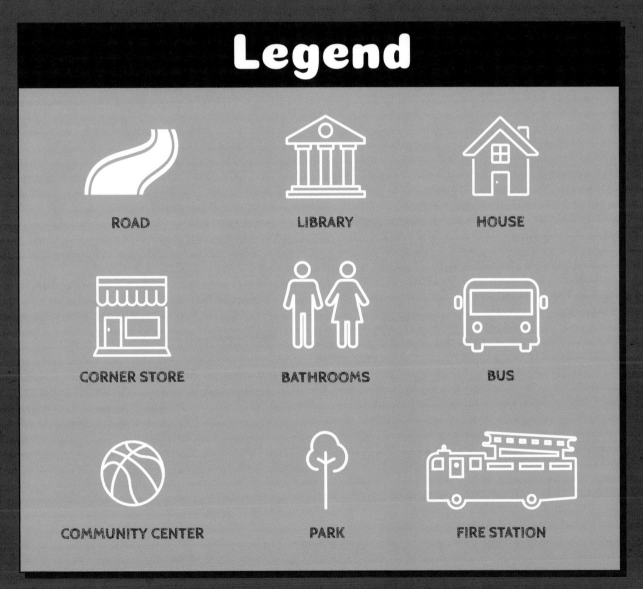

Legend

ROAD	LIBRARY	HOUSE
CORNER STORE	BATHROOMS	BUS
COMMUNITY CENTER	PARK	FIRE STATION

IS YOUR MAP COMPLETE?

Do not forget to add your legend, a title, and a compass rose to your community map.

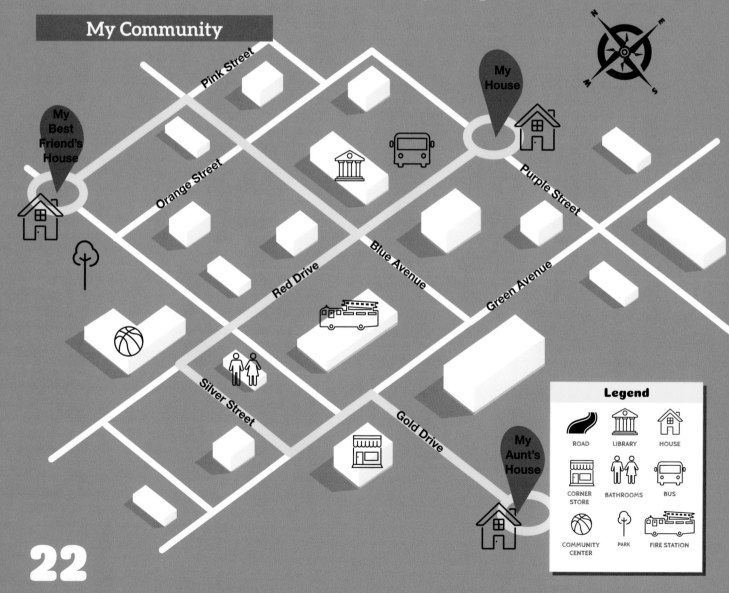

My Community

Pink Street

My Best Friend's House

Orange Street

My House

Purple Street

Blue Avenue

Red Drive

Green Avenue

Silver Street

Gold Drive

My Aunt's House

Legend

ROAD	LIBRARY	HOUSE
CORNER STORE	BATHROOMS	BUS
COMMUNITY CENTER	PARK	FIRE STATION

What points of interest would you add
to your community if you could?

Would you like to live next door
to a zoo? Add it to your map!

GLOSSARY AND INDEX

GLOSSARY

area A specific place, such as land

bird's-eye view Looking down on something from high above

community A group of people who live in the same area and share services

compass rose A map part that shows north, south, east, and west

digital Display using electronic or computer technology

distance Space between two points

landforms Features on Earth's surface formed by nature, such as mountains

legend A map part that lists symbols and their meanings

physical Something you can see and touch

political Relating to governments

scale The amount by which everything on a map has been shrunk so it fits on a page or screen

services Work provided to people

symbols A shape or picture that stands for a building, place, or other object

INDEX